Weird Creatures of the World

Tamara Einstein &
Einstein Sisters

KidsWorld

Weird
Creatures

The Earth is populated
by millions of creatures. We
know very little about most
of them. From single-celled
organisms to large mammals
and everything in between,
this book is full of weird
creatures.

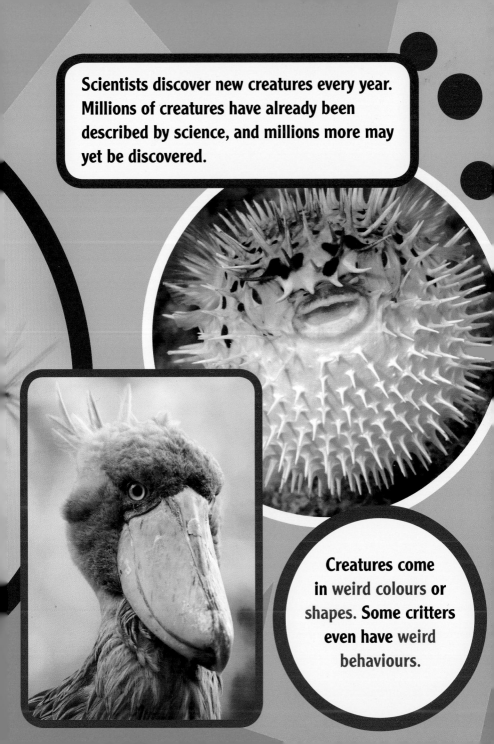

Scientists discover new creatures every year.
Millions of creatures have already been
described by science, and millions more may
yet be discovered.

Creatures come
in weird colours or
shapes. Some critters
even have weird
behaviours.

Sea Pen

Sea pens **look like plants growing on the ocean floor, but they are actually animals! One pen is a colony of many polyps, like tiny jellyfish with tentacles.**

Sea pens get their name because they look like old-fashioned feather pens in an ink pot.

If one of the polyps loses its tentacles, it becomes the main stem and base to which the other polyps attach. The supporting polyp is called the peduncle.

Peduncle

See the individual polyps up close.
In the center of each polyp is its mouth.

Glass Frog

Glass frogs are a group of frogs that live mainly in Central America. Females lay their eggs in trees above water. Males protect the eggs until they hatch, and the tadpoles fall into the water below.

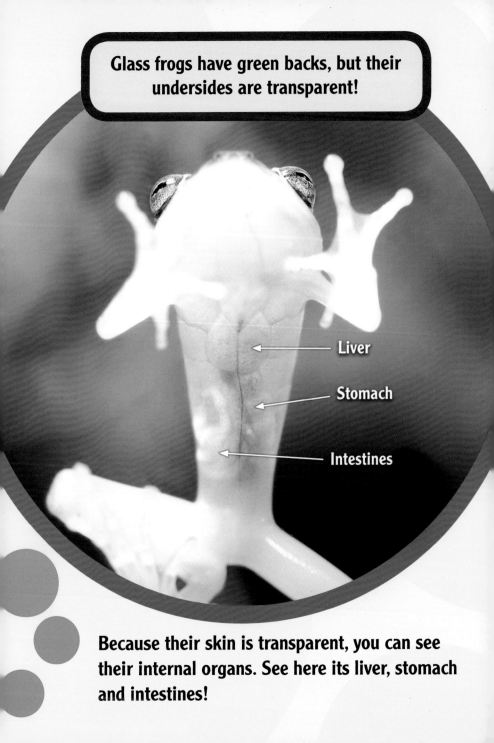

Glass frogs have green backs, but their undersides are transparent!

Because their skin is transparent, you can see their internal organs. See here its liver, stomach and intestines!

Weird Caterpillars

Caterpillars are the larva of butterflies and moths.

Cecropia

Saddleback

Dryandra

Sycamore

Caterpillars are eaten by many predators, such as birds and small mammals, so they need ways to defend themselves.

Frangipani

Leopard lacewing

Hickory Horned Devil

To **protect** themselves, some caterpillars are **poisonous**. Others have **hairs** that irritate the eyes or mouths of predators. Colorful caterpillars are often poisonous.

Spicebush Swallowtail

Lackey

Some caterpillars have big spots similar to eyes that make them look like snakes. Predators avoid snakes!

Hoatzin

One of the weirdest birds is the Hoatzin. It lives in the rainforest of South America. Young Hoatzins have moveable claws on the edges of their wings to help them climb around their nest.

Unlike other birds, the Hoatzin eats leaves. It has a digestive system that ferments vegetation much like a cow's does. They even smell a bit like cows!

Hoatzin chicks escape predators by jumping out of the nest. They climb back up to the nest using the claws on their feet and wings.

Sea Cucumber

Robust Sea Cucumber

These weird creatures look like colorful, bumpy vegetables, but sea cucumbers are really animals! They are related to starfish, sand dollars and sea urchins.

When a predator such as a crab or fish attacks, sea cucumbers can eject special sticky tubes into the water that entangle the predator while the sea cucumber escapes.

Black Sea Cucumber

Sea cucumbers move using thousand of tiny tube feet.

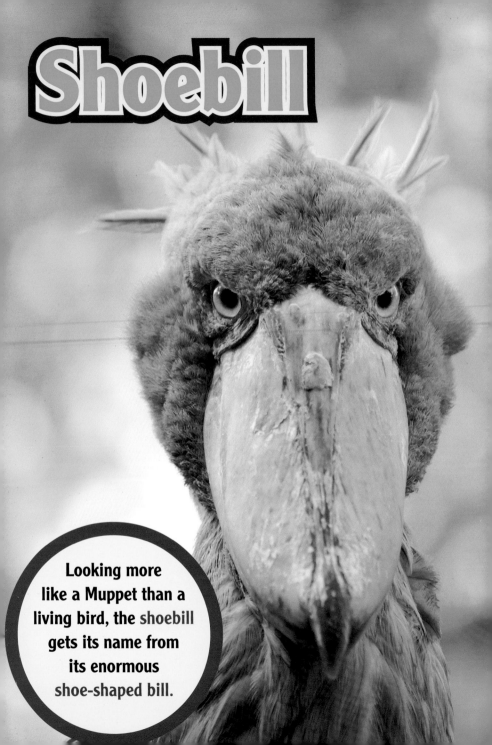

Shoebill

Looking more like a Muppet than a living bird, the shoebill gets its name from its enormous shoe-shaped bill.

The shoebill lives in the marshlands of central Africa.

It hunts by waiting motionless for fish to come to the water's surface. It's so good at not moving that many people say it looks like a statue. When it sees a fish, it snaps its head down and grabs it with its hooked bill.

Slime Mold

Slime molds are creatures that are neither plants nor animals nor true molds (fungi). Scientists don't really know how to describe them! Slime molds normally live as single-cells, but when food is scarce they can form a group and move as a single body in search of food.

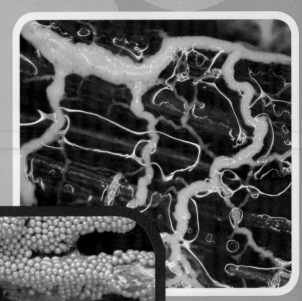

Slime molds feed on microscopic bacteria and fungi.

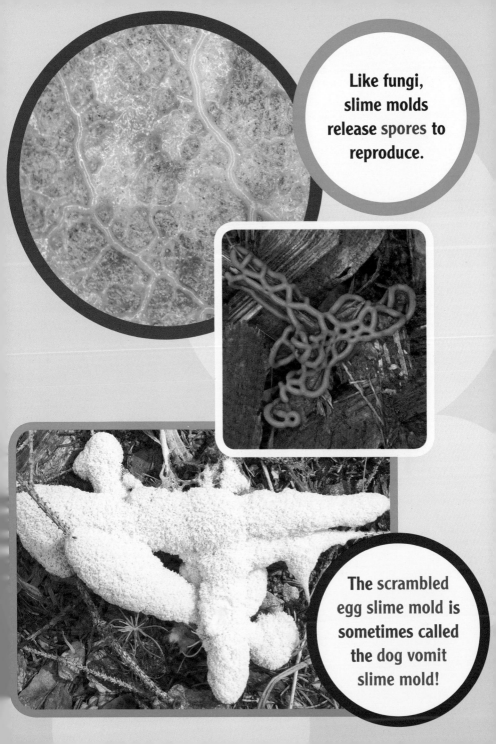

Like fungi, slime molds release spores to reproduce.

The scrambled egg slime mold is sometimes called the dog vomit slime mold!

Cassowary

The cassowary is a living bird that almost looks like a dinosaur. It can be as tall as a basketball player!

Casque

The casque is like a horn that grows on the top of their heads. It has hollow sections that amplify their calls in the rainforests of Australia and New Guinea.

A cassowary has legs and feet that are unusually large and powerful. The inner two toes each have a long dagger-like claw that the bird uses for defense. Although they are not normally aggressive, cassowaries have been known to kill humans and dogs.

Mantis

Mantises are insects with large arms, triangular heads and big eyes. Most mantises wait patiently for an insect to approach, then they quickly grab it with their large arms. They hold their prey tightly while eating it alive. Most mantises are camouflaged so they can hide among plants.

An orchid mantis is either pink or white so that it can hide among orchid flowers. It eats the insects that visit the flowers.

The wandering violin mantis is sometimes called a dead leaf mantis because it looks like a dried twig with leaves.

Jellyfish

Moon Jelly

Jellyfish are umbrella-shaped animals that live in the ocean. They have tentacles with thousands of tiny stingers that stun their prey, such as fish or shrimp.

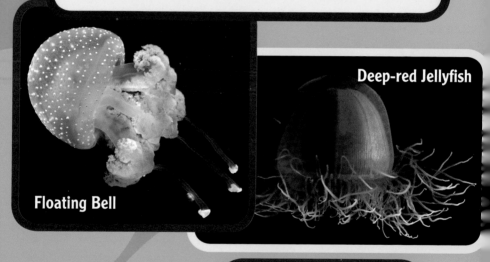

Deep-red Jellyfish

Floating Bell

Jellyfish can be longer than a blue whale, or as small as a grain of sand. The most deadly venom in the world is from a box jellyfish!

Box Jellyfish

Cauliflower Jellyfish

Jellyfish have have been alive for about 700 million years. That's a long time, even before dinosaurs!

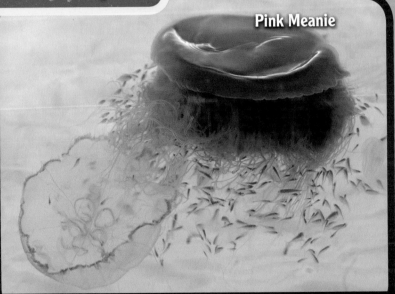

Pink Meanie

The pink meanie is a recently discovered species of giant jellyfish that feeds on other jellyfish! Little fish that are immune to the jellyfish's sting often swim under it for safety from predators. The little fish attract predators that the pink meanie then catches and eats. The little fish get to eat bits of the catch as well.

Lowland Streaked Tenrec

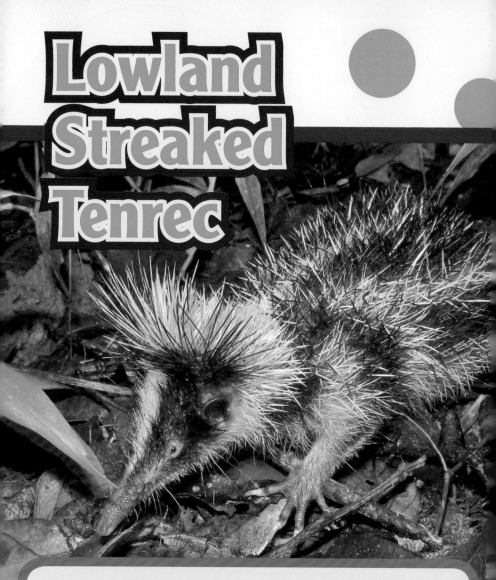

Covered in yellow and black bristles and spines, this unusual mammal lives only in Madagascar, an island off the west coast of Africa. The lowland streaked tenrec is the only mammal that can make sound and communicate to family members by rubbing together the spines on its back.

Lowland streaked tenrecs spend much of their lives burrowing in the soil looking for earthworms to eat. Sometimes they stomp their feet on the ground to encourage earthworms to come to the surface.

Pangolin

The pangolin is the only mammal that is covered in scales. They live in Asia and Africa.

Pangolins eat ants and termites. They feed by scratching open an anthill or termite mound and licking up the insects. Their tongues have sticky saliva to trap the insects.

Pangolins curl up into a ball to protect themselves from predators.

They have special muscles to close their ears and nostrils to keep the insects out.

A single pangolin can eat 20,000 ants in a day!

Sea Slugs

Sea slugs are also known as nudibranchs. They are like snails that no longer have shells. Sea slugs are mollusks, a group that includes snails, clams, octopuses and squid. There are thousands of different sea slugs!

Hypselodoris kanga

Spanish Shawl

Sea slugs are carnivores. They eat other animals like sea anemones, jellyfish and even other sea slugs!

Glossodoris atromarginata

Variable Neon Slug

Sea slugs have feathery external gills that look a bit like tentacles.

Chromodoris annae

Blue Dragon

The blue dragon feeds on jellyfish, even those with deadly stingers. The sea slugs store the stingers in their own bodies, making these sea slugs painful and dangerous to touch.

Sand Dollar

The sand dollar is an animal that is related to sea urchins, starfish and sea cucumbers. The hard shell is called a test, and it is covered with tiny bristles. A sand dollar has many tiny tube feet on its underside. Its mouth is in the center of the underside.

When feeding, sand dollars angle themselves in the sand so they can filter plankton from the water. They use their bristles and tube feet to move food to their mouths.

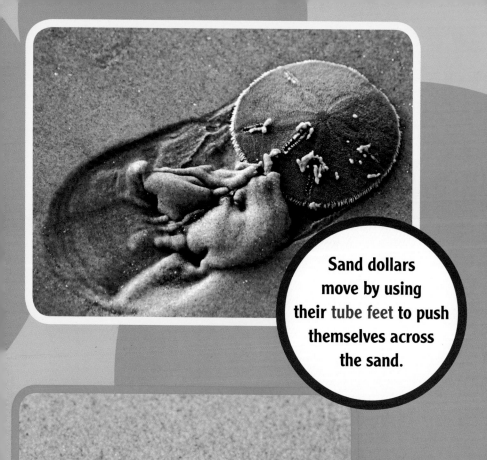

Sand dollars move by using their tube feet to push themselves across the sand.

When sand dollars die, they turn white and lose their bristles. White sand dollars are sometimes found on beaches. Legend says they are the lost coins of mermaids.

Net-casting Spider

Unlike all other spiders, net-casting spiders make stretchy webs that they hold with their 4 front legs.

Net-casting spiders hunt at night.

When a moth or other insect comes near these spiders, they can see it with their excellent night vision. They stretch the web wide and lunge forward, trapping their prey in their net.

Another name for this spider is the ogre-faced spider because of its large eyes and fangs!

Frogfish

Striated Frogfish

Frogfishes live in warm oceans around the world. They come in many colours and shapes that help them blend in to the coral reefs in which they live.

Clown Frogfish

Some frogfishes have spines and resemble sea urchins.

All frogfishes eat fish, shrimps and crabs. To catch their prey, they swim slowly toward the animal and then stop. When the prey approaches, they open their mouths very quickly to suck in the prey.

Striated Frogfish

Frogfishes have an antenna-like structure above their mouths, called an esca, that can be extended and wiggled to attract their prey.

Ocelated Frogfish

Gerenuk

A gerenuk is a type of antelope that lives in eastern Africa. It has an extremely long and skinny neck.

Males have curved and pointy horns.

Because of their long necks and ability to stand on their hind legs, gerenuks can feed on leaves high above ground!

The name gerenuk is a Somali word that means "giraffe-necked." Gerenuks are not related to giraffes.

Tardigrade

Tardigrades are micro-animals that live everywhere
on Earth, from the tops of volcanoes to the bottoms
of the deepest oceans and even the polar ice caps!
Tardigrades are also called water bears because they
walk slowly like a bear. Unlike real bears, however,
tardigrades have eight legs!

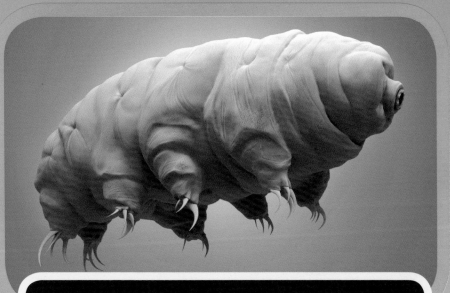

Tardigrades are extremophiles, meaning they can survive in extreme conditions. They can survive in space, extremely hot or cold temperatures, pollution, radiation and under extreme pressure.

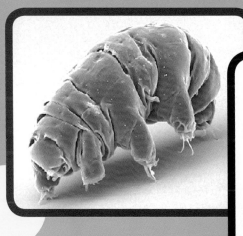

Tardigrades are among only a few creatures to have survived all five of the mass extinctions that have occurred on Earth, including the extinction event that killed off the dinosaurs.

Giant Anteater

Giant anteaters live in Central and South America. With narrow heads, pointed snouts, long tongues, hairy tails and white stripes, giant anteaters are weird!

Sometimes their black and white markings can make their front legs look like the head of a panda bear!

Giant anteaters are insectivores, meaning they feed entirely on insects such as ants and termites. They have no teeth. They collect insects with their long, sticky tongues and mash them against the roof of their mouths before swallowing.

Leaf-tailed Gecko

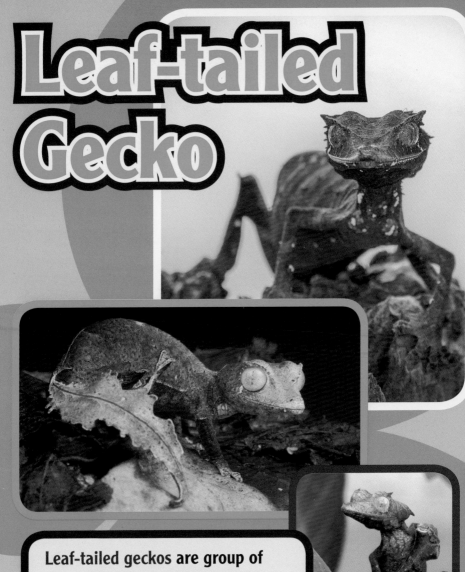

Leaf-tailed geckos are group of geckos that live in Madagascar, an island off the west coast of Africa. Like other geckos, they have no eyelids. They use their long tongues to lick their eyeballs clean!

Leaf-tailed geckos show amazing camouflage. Some of these geckos look like dry, brown leaves, while others look like tree bark. Some geckos are so well camouflaged that it is almost impossible to see them!

Leafy Sea Dragon

Leafy sea dragons are fish related to seahorses and pipefish. They live only on the southern coast of Australia. Leafy sea dragons have long, leafy branches on their bodies that help them hide in seaweed.

Like seahorses, males have a belly pouch into which the female lays her eggs. When the eggs hatch and leave the pouch, it looks like the male is giving birth.

Even though they are called dragons, the largest leafy sea dragons are no bigger than a piece of writing paper.

Leaf Insect

Leaf insects are found in South Asia and Australia. They look almost identical to tree leaves. They move very slowly, and when they walk they even wave back and forth so they appear to be leaves moving in the breeze.

Leaf insects can grow to be as large as an adult's hand.

Their camouflage protects them from predators like birds and lizards.

Coral

Corals live in warm oceans around the world. Although they look like colorful plants, they are actually animals.

Pink Finger Coral

Corals are related to jellyfish. One coral is like thousands of tiny jellyfish, called polyps, that live together. These animals live on the hard cases or branches that they build out of minerals.

A close-up of the surface of a coral shows the individual polyps with their tentacles extended. Polyps catch tiny organisms to eat. They feed by stinging prey with their tentacles and bringing the food to their central mouths.

Brain coral is a large coral that grows in reefs. The folds make it look like a brain!

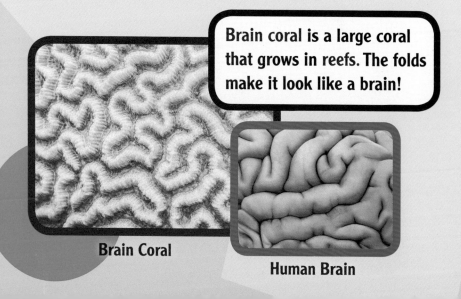

Brain Coral

Human Brain

Porcupinefish

Porcupinefish are found in warm oceans around the world. They live in coral reefs. Sometimes hundreds or even thousands can be found together in a school.

Porcupinefish can rapidly swallow water or air to inflate themselves. This protects them from predators such as sharks and dolphins because their spines stick straight out. Most predators will avoid trying to eat a puffed up porcupinefish!

Firefly

Confusingly, fireflies are beetles, not flies. There are many kinds of fireflies that live around the world. Fireflies have special organs in their abdomens that produce light.

Some fireflies produce a constant light while they fly.

Other firelies produce light that blinks on and off while they fly.

Different species of fireflies can produce various colors of light. Some may be yellow, green, pale red or even blue.

Fireflies mainly use the light to attract a mate.

Dinoflagellates

Dinoflagellates **are** microcellular organisms **that live** in both saltwater and freshwater habitats.

Many species of ocean dinoflagellates can emit light when they are disturbed. Waves on the shore and boats often cause them to light up.

The light emitted by dinoflagellates is either blue or greenish.

The main purpose of the glow is for defense. If a predator swims through the dinoflagellates, the flash of light may startle it so it swims away. If not, the predator is highlighted and becomes more visible to even larger predators that may then attack it.

Dugong & Manatee

Dugong

Dugongs and manatees are marine mammals that live in shallow water. Dugongs feed on marine plants, making them the only completely vegetarian marine mammal. Manatees eat plants, too, but also some crabs, clams and fish.

Dugong

Manatee

Manatees have paddle-like tails, while a dugong has a tail shaped like a dolphin's. Dugongs also have a larger snout than manatees.

Manatee Toenails

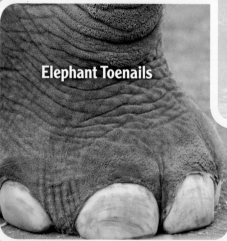

Elephant Toenails

Dugongs and manatees are related to elephants. Their toenails are very similar!

Glowworm

Glowworms are not really worms. They are the larval stage of an insect called a fungus gnat. They live on the roof of caves in New Zealand.

Glowworms secrete strings of silk with sticky beads, called snares, that hang around them. These beads glow to attract their prey. Mosquitos and moths fly toward them and get stuck in the snares. The larvae can then eat them.

The hungrier the larvae, the more brightly they glow!

Swell Shark

Swell sharks
get their name from
their ability to swallow
water and "swell" to nearly
twice their size. This is
a defense against larger
predators.

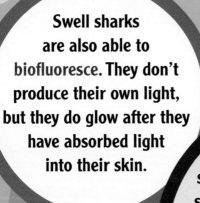

Swell sharks are also able to biofluoresce. They don't produce their own light, but they do glow after they have absorbed light into their skin.

Their glow is similar to glow-in-the-dark stickers that only glow after you shine light on them. Researchers think the light is a form of communication and maybe even helps with camouflage.

Thorny Devil

The thorny devil
is a lizard that lives in the
deserts of Australia. It is
covered in sharp spikes. The
spikes keep it safe.
Most predators will
avoid trying to eat
this lizard!

Thorny devils can drink by touching any part of their body to water. Ridges in their scales carry the water to their mouths. In the same way, they can drink the dew that collects on their scales overnight.

The Publisher: KidsWorld Books

Library and Archives Canada Cataloguing in Publication

Einstein, Tamara, author
 Weird Creatures of the World / Tamara Einstein & Einstein Sisters.
ISBN 978-1-988183-48-0 (softcover) ISBN 978-1-988183-49-7 (epub)
  1. Animals—Miscellanea—Juvenile literature. 2. Exotic animals—
Miscellanea—Juvenile literature. I. Einstein Sisters, author II. Title.
QL49.E42 2019   j590   C2018-905985-0
                                                 C2018-905986-9

Front cover: From Thinkstock, yod67.

Back cover: From Thinkstock: Howard Chen, lilithlita, JohnCarnemolla.

Photo credits: From Thinkstock: 630ben, 26-27; ABDESIGN, 7; Andrea Izzotti, 56b; Anolis01, 18; artas, 20b; AtanasBozhikovNasko, 55b; atese, 4; baihoen, 53a; barbaraaaa, 45b; bugking88, 29b; Byrdyak, 36b; CathyKeifer, 9c, 20a; cbpix, 28a; Chris Watson, 63a; Cindy Chow, 45a; Comstock Images, 13c; Connah, 11a; Daniel Haesslich, 26; DariaRen, 8d; Dorling Kindersley, 11b; Eraxion, 49c; espencer1, 31b; fruttipics, 39a; FtLaudGirl, 3a, 51; Gaardman, 10; goir, 5b; hakoar, 25b; Iuliia Morozova, 16a, 17ab; JanelleLugge, 63b; joebelanger, 28b; JohnCarnemolla, 62-63; Jupiterimages, 9a; Kesu01, 3b, 14; kororokerokero, 52a; Kyslynskyy, 36a, 37; LauraDin, 56a; LeaveWithSteve, 34a; lirtlon, 46ab; lues01, 15a; macro frog insect animal, 21a; MarcelStrelow, 58-59; Martin Wheeler, 9d; Massimo_S8, 42a; mlharing, 57a; Musat, 41b; mychadre77, 48a; N-sky, 50b; naturediver, 5a, 12a; oceanbounddb, 13a; Ocs_12, 18; Oleksii Spesyvtsev, 50a; olga_steckel, 23b; Placebo365, 49b; plovets, 12b; redchanka, 47; reptiles4all, 6a, 25a, 42b; RibeirodosSantos, 34b; ruiruito, 53b; sihasakprachum, 52b; thomasmales, 9e; tingfen, 44b; VanessaVolk, 40a; vlad61, 48b; watcherFF, 54; webguzs, 33b; williamhc, 45c; yod67, 2, 9b. From Wikimedia Commons: Aditya Sainiarya, 38; Alextelford, 42c; Bjørn Christian Tørrissen, 19a; Chan siuman, 30; Chen-Pan Liao, 33ac; Chika Watanabe, 28c; Christophe Germain, 43a; D Ross Robertson, 60a; Derek Keats, 23a; Ellen, 40b; Francesco Veronesi, 43b; Frank Vassen, 24; Fritz Geller-Grimm 57b; Gerald J. Lenhard, 8b; Guido Gautsch, 22d; Hans Hillewaert, 22a; Hexasoft, 43c; Jens Peterson, 35a; John Tann, 8c; John Tracy, 31a; Judy Gallagher, 32; Lebrac, 16b; Malene Thyssen, 41a; Maria Antónia Sampayo, Instituto de Oceanografia, Faculdade Ciências da Universidade de Lisboa , 55a; Markrosenrosen, 59b; Mauricio Rivera Correa, 6b; Michael Hodge, 8a; Mnolf, 59a; Nhobgood, 29a; Nick Hobgood, 5c, 35b; NOAA, 22c, 49a; Orest, 22b; pelican, 15b; Psych USD, 57c; Rpillon, 13b; Sandip kumar, 27c; Schokraie E, Warnken U, Hotz-Wagenblatt A, Grohme MA, Hengherr S, et al. (2012), 39b; Scott Hamlin, 19b; Shantanu Kuveskar, 21b; Siga, 17c; Sparks, J. S.; Schelly, R. C.; Smith, W. L.; Davis, M. P.; Tchernov, D.; Pieribone, V. A.; Gruber, D. F., 60-61; Sylke Rohrlach, 29c, 44a; USFWS, 27b.

We acknowledge the financial support of the Government of Canada.
Nous reconnaissons l'appui financier du gouvernement du Canada.

Funded by the Government of Canada
Financé par le gouvernement du Canada | Canadä

PC: 38